CW00968117

The Hidden Secrets and Treasures of Having Fun on and Around the Ski Resorts

A Quick Guide:

- The definition of Fun
- How to achieve Fun
- Treasure hunt for seeking Fun
- Keepsake of Fun memories
- Closure

Dr. Herbert K. Naito

508 West 26th Street KEARNEY, NE 68848
402-819-3224
info@medialiteraryexcellence.com

Table of Contents

Something about the Author

He spent 40 years in the medical profession. For fun, he coached skiing for over 20 years. He is a member of the Professional Ski Instructors of America, and is certified in Alpine Skiing, Level 2; Adaptive Specialist, Level 1; Children's Specialist, Level 2; Senior Specialist, Level 2; and Children's Trainer. Currently he is employed by the Vail Ski Resorts and is presently on the Vail Educational Staff. He was the former Director of the Children's Advanced Training Specialist, and the Express Pre-School School Ski Programs.

In addition to this book, he has written six other books on skiing:

"A Comprehensive Guide for Coaching Children How To Ski"

"How to Prepare for your Child's First Ski Lesson"

"The Funky Donkey Tells His Story About His First Ski Lesson"

"Coaching Wacky Raccoon, Children, and Adults the Fundamentals of Good Sportsmanship"

"How to Create Fun for Children with Disabilities on the Ski Slopes"

"How to Create a Successful Ski Lesson for Senior Citizens"

This book was supported by a generous grant from the Dr. and Mrs.

Herbert K. Naito Charitable Foundation Grant.

Definition of Fun

Fun can mean many things to many people, like 50 Shades of Gray. It can depend on a person's ethnic background, educational level, personal experiences, mental attitude, and physical experiences and background. Your childhood development and exposure to activities have a role in your adult behavior and definition of fun. For example, if you grew up surrounded by farmers, you will more than likely have an interest in farm-related activities. If your dad was not a handyman, you probably have little interest with building a treehouse and would not consider it a fun activity.

So, what is fun? The dictionary defines *fun* as amusement, entertainment, merriment, pleasure, joking, playful. So, that is a whole lot of words that mean many things to different people.

What is the opposite of fun? How about boredom? The definition of bore is being weary, dull, uninteresting, or monotonous. When you go out on a family outing or vacation, which of the two, fun or boredom, would you choose? Well, it depends on your objective and mission.

How to Achieve Fun

It starts with your mind. According to a clinical psychologist, your moods, temperament, attitudes can be controlled by positive thinking. People who think positively about their future, who believe they can control their outcomes, and who are willing to open and share with others are healthier individuals. The power of positive thinking comes in different forms, but they are all helpful. Some researchers have focused on optimism, a general tendency to expect positive outcomes. Other researchers have focused on self-efficacy; the belief in our ability to carry out actions that produce desired outcomes. Folks with high self-efficacy respond to environmental and other threats in an active, constructive way by obtaining information, talking to friends, and by attempting to face and reduce the difficulties they are experiencing.

Your mental attitude will be the driving force to achieving fun. If you start out with not being motivated or excited about the activity, the chance for achieving fun will diminish no matter how exciting and adventurous the planned venture is. An entertainer could be standing on his/her head, and you will demonstrate weariness and being uninterested. This type of mental attitude, will drag the rest of the accompanying group down; it's like a viral pandemic outbreak (See figure 1). So, shift your gear into a positive mode, an adventurous mode, a mode of excitement and fun.

Figure 1. This boy's mind is not in a positive mode. To have fun on this trip he needs to change his attitude.

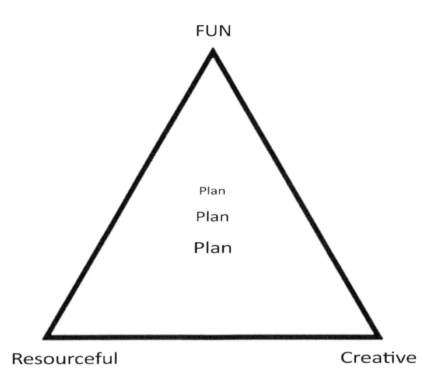

Figure 2. The ingredients for having fun. The major ingredient is planning, planning, planning. Sprinkle creativity and resourcefulness to be successful.

Achieving fun does not just happen. It takes planning, planning, planning (See figure 2). Besides a lot of careful planning, you will need creativity, resourcefulness, and adventurous curiosity. These are the must-have ingredients for a successful vacation trip. I will provide you with a laundry list of adventures when you go on a ski trip and stay at a ski resort. I will start the list with some benign activities and end with more unique and adventurous venues. Besides searching the internet, you can always ask the concierge at the hotel for local information. Families, couples, singles appear to get restless with just skiing the local ski resorts. The news media and smart phones play a role in yearning to see other countries. Today's, vacationers have the resources, the finance, and motivation to fly to different states to ski and ride. Some will do the 10 provinces of Canada for some fabulous and adventuresome skiing; some will even do transpacific, transatlantic, and transpolar flights.

If you're taking the time, money, and resources to travel, why not add other activities to your agenda to make it more fulfilling, exciting and fun? I hear people always saying, *"Life is too short; I need to live life to the fullest."* I have added a treasure chest next to the sub topic that is worthy of trying on your vacation.

Treasure Hunt of Fun

Indoor activities

If your objective is to relax after a hard-day skiing, then pick up a book that you have been wanting to read. Or finish crocheting a sweater for your grandchild. Or play checkers, chess, or cards if they relax you. You might do yourself a favor by turning your mobile phone off during your "quiet time," and only turn it on a couple of hours. You need to be disciplined to stick to your mission for a relaxing vacation. It might also be a good time to catch up on communications, to catch up on knitting, on reading a book.

Photo 1. This young happy lady is cozy and immersing herself in her favorite book with a hot chocolate.

Spas and Wellness Centers

When you go to a high-end ski resort, there are more amenities. Today's spas and wellness centers are more sophisticated with holistic treatments, saunas of different types, steam rooms for different purposes, hydro pools and hot-springs thermal spas for therapeutic uses. The rooms are posh with a beautiful ambiance, filled with candles with different fragrances, and music to relax you. You will certainly feel like a King or Queen for a day. You will be transfixed into a winter wonderland of pleasure and relaxation. They have certified nutritionists and dietitians that can analyze and plan a weight-reduction or gain weight program for you. They may have cosmetologists that can study your skin's needs and formulate holistic concoctions that will inspire you to take better care of you skin in the harsh winter weather. They have trained experts on facial and body massages. In general, a standard visit to the spa will cost $150-$500.

Photo 2. This young lady is having a full facial treatment at a high end spa.

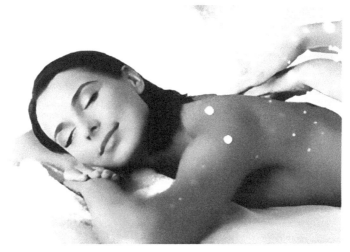

Photo 3. This young lady is indulging in a total body massage for a full relaxation.

Ski Clubs

One of the best advices that I can give you is to join a local ski club. They are geared for social activities; some clubs support their club race team to compete with other club race teams.

They arrange bus trips and flights to other states and *continents. Most of the time it is more fun to go with a large group of friends. As they say, "There is strength in numbers; there's more brain power to get more ideas flowing, more physical power to get the job done, and more emotional power to get your anxieties and frustrations resolved."*

In addition, you will develop lots of friends, which will make any event and activity more fun. Do not underestimate the power of ski clubs. Scales of economies always tips the scale into your favor when it comes to cost.

Photo 4. A group of friends from a ski club are having a few refreshments to enjoy each other's company after a hard-day skiing.

Dress Code

Other than the standard ski outfit, you may want to be more adventurous and dress in a clown or bikini outfit. Ski clubs tend to create themes for their ski trips.

Photo 5. A group of ski club members wanted to goof around on the ski slopes in their clown outfits.

Photo 6. A young girl from a ski club is in a bikini outfit to join her teammates from her ski club.

Fireplace

Another relaxing activity; yes, it is another great indoor activity. But you can ramp it up by partaking in some local wine to add to the relaxing musical atmosphere. Some ski resorts or larger hotel complexes will have outdoor fireplaces and refreshments served during specific hours of the evening.

Photo 7. A young lady is enjoying her Merlot wine next to an indoor fireplace at her ski lodge room.

Bonfire

To help get rid of trash in rural France, they burned bones to enrich the fertilizer. Thus, it was called bone fire; over time, it was later called "bon" or good fire. Now the word was transformed to bonfire. If you want a bit more solitude and independence, a bonfire might be your cup-of-tea. Be sure to practice safety and be informed about the ground rules for building a bonfire at the camp site.

Photo 8. A gentleman is serenading his girlfriend in front of a bonfire.

Hot tub

After a rigorous day of powder skiing, a hot tub is just the Rx you needed. Hot tubs can be indoors or outdoors. If you want to add class to your adventure, use one made out of special wood to release an aroma to add some spice into the atmosphere. You can modify by renting thermo-Spas with bubbles or a Jacuzzi tub. Spice it up by drinking some *"tiny bubbles"* also called Champagne. Your challenge is not going into the tub, but coming out of the tub and runnin back to your hotel room without getting frostbitten on the delicate parts of your body!

Photo 9. The Hot Tub challenge is to not get frostbitten running back to your hotel ski lodge room!

Unique meals

Try to make every attempt to seek local meals, whether it be smoked salmon, venison, or bison. Many high-end ski resorts employ four and five-star chefs rather than simply cooks to furnish remarkable and rememberable meals.

Photo 10. Many high-end resorts have 5-star Chefs rather than just cooks to provide you specular romantic candlelight dinners.

Snow tubing

The tubing size will differ depending on the facility. There are tubing for, single-, double-, or larger groups and the steepness will vary. Always be mindful that fun comes after safety in all activities that you participate in. It has been documented that neck whiplash and neck injuries have happened when the tubing overturned or crashed into an object. Dress properly according to the weather. Be mindful that your clothing, gloves and headgear are warm, waterproof, and breathable. Depending on the size of the tubing and ski resort location, the cost will vary from $30 to $45 for a two-hour ride of fun.

Photo 11. Take a break from skiing and try snow tubing down the hill.

Snowball fights

This is an inexpensive activity, but it requires some degree of caution. Be safe and wear some eye protection. Since they are readily available, wear your ski goggles for protection. For the little ones, aim the snowball below the head to prevent any accidents. Wear warm, waterproof, breathable gloves. Be mindful about frostnip and frostbite. The symptoms for frostnip are red skin turning whiter or paler, losing the sensation of cold, increasing pain. Do not sit by the fireplace to warm up; use warm blankets and warm beverages to warm up. After rewarming, the discolored and blistered skin will eventually scab over. It will heal over the six-month period.

Photo 12. Have some fun by having a family snowball fight to help create bonding.

Pets

Many hotels and motels may allow you to bring your pooch. Do inquire before you leave for your trip and follow the pet rules to not offend anyone. When at a pet-friendly hotel, check for any restrictions for your four-legged guests. Inquire about the pet fee, a pet-friendly room (Not all rooms are pet-friendly), bring your pet's own bed, and obey other rules that may be hidden in the contract. Keep barking to a minimum, especially late at night or early in the morning! Not everyone is a bright, rise and shine person. Many others staying at the hotel are on a relaxing vacation and their wake-up alarm is set at noon.

Photo 13. Bring some extra fun by bringing pooch along.

Sleigh ride and sledding

This is a fun sport for all ages. If the hotel does not have a rental program, check with the concierge. For some of the more unusual activities, check with the Tourist Information stations or with AAA. There are some hotels that will provide a large-carrying capacity sled that can shuttle you to various restaurants located at their ski resort.

Photo 14. Have you ever tried Tobogganing? Like tubing, you have no directional control with Tobogganing.

Photo 15. Look at the two kids' faces; you think they're having a blast riding the Sleigh?

Photo 16. Especially around Christmas, you should make every attempt to arrange for a large sleigh ride with a large group of friends.

Sunbathing

There are many ways of exposing your skin to the rays. You need sunscreen at that altitude. Research indicates that for every 1,000 feet of elevation, the solar UV rays intensify by eight- to ten percent because of the thinning of the atmosphere. As a consequence, people, especially young children get sunburns more quickly and more severely. As compared to sea level, an 8,000 feet elevation exposes a person to about 25 percent more ultraviolet radiation. Protect your skin with hydration and moisturizing products. The low humidity of the high-mountain air can leave your skin feeling itchy, sensitive and dry. Drink a lot of plain water; limit your intake of coffee and tea because they are diuretic agents that will actually leave you more dehydrated.

Photo 17. A young lady in a bathing suit getting a sun tan. You think she needs lots of suntan lotion?

Building a Snowman

This is a fun thing for the whole family. You might do this in the early evening so you don't utilize all your precious time for skiing. Don't forget the carrot, two brown cookies, a long liquorish candy, scarf, hat and couple of branch twigs.

Photo 18. Build bonding by building a large snowman. Don't forget the carrot, scarf, hat, two cookies, and few branches.

Snowshoeing and Hiking

Besides breathing the fresh mountain air, there are many health benefits of snowshoeing such as increasing cardiovascular fitness, building muscular tone, increasing neuromuscular coordination, and burning calories for weight reduction. For the latter effects, according to the University of Vermont, you can burn between 420-1000 calories per hour. It burns twice the number of calories as walking at the same speed. If you want to set the torch on fire, pick up the pace and increase the incline of the hill. Rental cost for the ski boots, poles and skis, is approximately $50 to $75 per day. Practice safety by going in small groups, go during daylight hours, wear sunglasses to avoid the bright glare, and carry a water bottle to prevent dehydration in the dry altitude.

Photo 19. How about going snowshoeing after your first cut of coffee and smell all that fresh pine scent?

Cross-Country Skiing

Like snowshoe and hiking, cross-country hiking provides the same physical benefits. Both sports will give mental relief too. According to Harvard Public Health, a 125-pound person who spends 60 minutes cross-country skiing burns 480 calories, and a 185- pound male will burn 710 calories. Rental equipment is abundant; the cost is about the same as snowshoeing. The cost for snow is extra!

Photo 20. How about trying something different such as cross-country skiing?

Curling

Curling is a sport in which players slide granite stones (Called the Rock) on a sheet of ice toward a target area, which is segmented into four concentric circles (Called the House). It is related to shuffleboard. In the traditional ten-end games, each team receives 38 minutes thinking time. This is reduced to 30 minutes for eight-end games. The curlers sweep the ice to help the stone travel further and straighter or in a direction you want the rock to go. Sweeping in front of the stone reduces the friction and helps the curlers control the amount of curl the stone undergoes. If they want a stone to travel farther with less curl, they sweep more. For all your history buffs, Scotland came up with the Rules in Curling and the Curling Club was formed in 1838. There is a lot of yelling in this game; like "hurry" which means to sweep as fast as possible; or "hurry hard," which means to sweep quickly and apply downward pressure; and "clean," which means to keep the broom on the ice with minimal pressure in order to make sure nothing impedes the stone's path. There are four members to each team and the captain is called "Skip."

Photo 21. How about trying something totally different like Curling. It is a lot of fun. Besides, you will become a better sweeper for your home with some practice.

Fat Biking

Fat bike is an off-road bicycle with oversized tires, designed for low ground pressure to allow riding on soft, unstable terrain such as snow, sand, slush, bogs, and mud. Staying fit in the winter is hard, but these specially-designed bikes make outdoor exercise not only possible, but also fun. On a fat bike, you can burn up to 1,500 calories and hour in soft conditions. You'll recover faster with less low-back pain than a long run. Like all bicycles, you need to be properly fitted to gain maximum power, be more efficient during the peddling phase, and safer. These mountain bikes are pricier rentals than a single speed road bike, which is no surprise. Yet, even among mountain bikes there are more expensive variants. The length of time (Half-day or full-day) for the rental is another factor for the cost, which can be $50-$75 for ½ day and $150-$200 for a full day. Don't forget to rent a helmet to protect your noodle!

Photo 22. Fat Biking is getting to be very popular in the winter; it is a great way to have fun and lose weight.

Dog Sledding

A dog sled or dog sleigh is a sled pulled by one or more sled dogs over ice and through snow. There are numerous types of sleds, designed with different functions. There are several places that will rent a dog sled with sled dogs: Alaska, Colorado, Pennsylvania, New York, Wisconsin, Maine, Michigan, Minnesota, Montana, Utah. Why is the cost of rentals so high? It's not so much for the cost of the sled and related equipment, but for maintaining the sled dogs all year around. You may also want a tour guide to assist you with managing the team of unfamiliar dogs. A snowmobile only needs a garage! For a ½-day trip, Kids (5-11 years-old) is $200-$300; Youth (12-17 years-old) is $250-$500; and adults $300-$600. For a full day, it is roughly double the ½-day price with a lumberjack lunch and beverage thrown in. Be sure to check if there are Veteran's or senior discounts.

Photo 23. They claim that dog sledding is a blast and everyone should try it at least once.

Ice Skating

Ice skating is the self-propulsion and gliding of a person across an ice surface, using metal-bladed ice skates. An average person burns 640-850 calories per hour skating on the ice. You have a choice of indoor or outdoor rinks. Some ski resorts may have ice skating rinks; or a private establishment may be locally available with a rental program. The cost is similar to going bowling.

Photo 24. Ice Skating is an entertaining sport that the entire family can enjoy.

Ice Fishing

If you are an avid fisherman or fisherwoman, ice fishing may be your thing for fun entertainment. Ask the residents about safety of the lake and what's biting. Safety and local fishing laws should be adhered to. Don't forget your ice drill, bait, and fishing license.

Photo 25. There are tons of frozen lakes around ski resorts. Be sure that you have your fishing license, bait, and a drill.

Fly Fishing

Fish do slow down during the winter months, but they never stop eating! Everything that I mentioned under ice fishing applies to fly fishing. Fly fishing is an angling method that uses a light-weight lure called an artificial fly to catch fish. The fly is casted using a long fly rod, reel, and specialized weighted line. This sport will test your patience. It is difficult enough to get the fly line out there onto the open water, but with pinpoint accuracy where the fish are located is another chapter to write about. In addition, do pack enough patients on your fly-fishing trip when untangling your fly from the tree tops.

Photo 26. Ski resorts are surrounded by outstanding fly fishing streams. Bring your fishing license, your favorite flies, and lots of patience untangling your fishing line from the trees.

Ice Yachting

This sport is also called iceboating. If you love the sport of sailing in the lake or ocean, you might want to try this. Iceboating is a recreational or competition sailing craft supported on metal runners for traveling over ice. One of the runners is steerable. The cost around $60,000-$60,000. Perhaps you're more interested in a rental; about $600 to $1500 per day. Better yet, go to a local yacht club and ask there is anyone who is interested in taking you on a spin on the ice. Don't forget the weather forecast before you book a rental.

Photo 27. If you're an avid sailor, try ice yachting. Check the weather forecast for the wind velocity.

Yoga

This might be a group class held at the ski resort or you can do it by yourself at the top of the mountain overlooking a panoramic view of the whole mountain range. There are eleven types of yoga: Vinyasa (The most athletic yoga); Hatha (Classic approach to breathing and exercises); Iyengar (Long-posing yoga); Kundalini (Equal part spiritual and physical); Asthtanga (A very physically demanding sequence of postures); Bikram (Poses in a sauna room with 105 degrees temperature and 45 percent humidity); Yin (Slow-paced style in a seated postures for a long time); Restorative (Focuses on winding down after a long day); Prenatal (Tailored for pregnant mothers); Anusara (Focus on alignment with more on the mind-body-heart connections); Jivamukti (Focus is on Hindu spiritual teachings and the earth). Yoga has many healthful advantages, but in short, peace of the mind, body and soul.

Photo 28. Outside yoga is entirely different. You not only sample the fresh air and get the panoramic views but also the weather elements when it is snowing. Dress Warm!

Bird Watching

For animal lovers, you may take advantage of bird watching in another state, country, or continent. There are roughly 10,000 bird species recorded in North America. Do not forget to bring your binoculars and bird-identification handbook.

Photo 29. Being at 11,000 feet up in a new geographic location bring you a smorgasbord of new birds to observe.

Museum

If you desire a more intellectual-life style on your vacation, try a museum. You can ask the local people or concierge for good advice.

There are 35,144 museums in the USA and over 95,000 in the world. Don't let all that treasure just sit there collecting dust!

Photo 30. With museums in every major city, do not miss the opportunity to see one that you have never seen—especially famous ones in Europe.

Winter Zoo

Winter is a great time to escape from the summer weather and crowds. There is usually a reduction in admission fees. Be sure to check the winter hours. There are over 2,800 zoos in the USA and over 10,000 zoos world-wide. Why don't you beat the heat and crowds by visiting the zoo during the winter?

Photo 31. Few people visit the zoo during the Winter—why not? Take the time and your children will enjoy the new experiences.

A Winter Winery and Beer Brewery Tour

This should be a popular tour. There are many outstanding wineries and breweries in this country and abroad. Even though it is winter, be sure to check for reservations and if they are serving the beverage. Check to see if they are also serving appetizers; some wineries and breweries do for a minimal fee.

Photo 32. Visit a winter winery and observe how they make their wines and taste their outcomes.

Photo 33. Friends are tasting different Brewery products.

Snowmobiling

Snowmobiling, also known as a motor sled, motor sledge, skimobile, snow scooter, Ski-Doo, or snowmachine, is a motorized vehicle designed for winter travel and recreation on snow and ice. The average weight is about 500 pounds, which can achieve speeds of 150 MPH. It can be a single- or double-passenger sled. Although this sport is not a completely high-risk activity, it is one of the most dangerous outdoor recreational activities. However, it can be safer when safety precautions are followed, including wearing a helmet. The frontal lobe of the brain (For wisdom and reasoning) is fully matured by age 25 year of age. Don't be one of those adults where the frontal lobe never matures!

Photo 34. After a hard day skiing, the group hired a tour guide for an early evening snowmobiling.

Winter-hang Gliding

It may seem that it is cold flying in an open cockpit when it is freezing out there. It may appear that winter is not the time to go hang gliding. WRONG! Technology has advanced; the heating system used by the military have been adapted to heating the clothing, gloves, boots, and vests. The gloves are 22 watts, boots are 22 watts, and vests are 44 watts. Winter flying is great because you can fly all day without the summer thermals that cause turbulence during the afternoon. Before you book a lesson, check for winter storms, which are more abundant than the summer.

Photo 35. Ever want to try Winter-Hang Gliding? Check the weather forecast; Avoid any thunder storms or rains.

Winter Golfing

Yup, there are a few nuts that can't stand to be locked up indoors during the winter and prefer the sunshine, fresh air, and the fun of golfing. The biggest thing you can do to get ready is to stay prepared; be ready for anything. Be prepared for the blast of snow, wind, and sleet. Keep warm and dress in layers. I use a heated glove and heated and waterproof golf shoes. I spend more time warming up and stretching those tight muscles and get the blood flowing. Understand the inter golf rules. Be prepared to walk rather than ride a cart. You will lose distance on your drives; adjust your woods by using ones with increasing loft. Other than that, just have *FUN*. By the way, you might want to use a brightly colored golf ball instead of a white ball.

Photo 36. Many skiers are truly nuts when it comes to golfing. When you go winter golfing, be sure to bring other than white balls.

Racing

There is a nonprofessional racing organization called NASTAR (**NA**tional **STA**ndard **R**ace) that you can participate. Your racing category will be based on your age and be compared to the national average. The data will be collected and kept on file to determine if you qualify for the national competition nationwide in Utah during the spring.

Photo 37. Pre-teen racer.

Photo 38. Teen racer with good racing fundamentals.

Photo 39. An older woman racing with more refined racing fundamentals.

Freestyle Skiing

This is a fun place to do your jumps, riding the rails, doing the tables, and the half-pipes. If you're new to this sport, get a certified freestyle ski instructor to teach you some of the basic moves and all of the safety rules.

Photo 40. Young boy in the Terrain Park showing good jumping fundamentals.

Photo 41. Immediate freestyle skier in terrain park.

Photo 42. Advanced freestyle skier in terrain park.

Winter Hot-Air Balloon

A hot-air balloon is often called an envelope, which contains heated air. Suspended beneath is a gondola or wicker basket that carries people. Liquid propane is used as the gas to ignite the flames to cause the hot air to rise. Modern balloons have been made in many shapes, such as rocket ships and shapes of various commercial products. From a statistical point, the FAA finds hot-air balloon the safest form of all air travel and rarely involved in aviation crashes. Hot- air balloon pilots don't have a steering wheel and use the winds at various levels to control the balloon's direction. The pilots fly within two hours of sunrise and two hours of sunset because the winds are the calmest and most consistent. There are festivals all over the world and the largest is in Albuquerque, New Mexico. There are states that you can rent winter hot-air balloons: Arizona, California, Colorado, Georgia, Idaho, Illinois, Iowa, Maryland, New Mexico, Nevada, New York, Ohio, Pennsylvania, South Dakota, Tennessee, Washington, Wisconsin. The cost is around$150-$300 per person on up, depending on the size of the basket and number of people riding. Pickups at your ski resort are available.

Photo 43. Try a spectacular Winter Hot Air Balloon ride 15,000 feet up above.

Motorcycle Riding in the Slush or Snow

For a change of pace, try riding a dirt bike in the snow. This is one sport that you need to be safety conscious at all times. Do wear a helmet, gloves and a shin guard. There are motorcycle clubs that have race courses set up that you can rent for a nominal fee.

Photo 44. Try riding a motorcycle in the ice slush. Wear a helmet and shin-guards!

Winter Conference

There are many organizations that schedule their conference at a ski resort so they can partake skiing (Or do the many exciting and adventurous activities that I've listed in this book) after their business or academic conference is accomplished.

Photo 45. *"Kill two birds with one stone." Do the business meeting lectures in the evening and go skiing during the day!*

Photo 46. *This young lady just hit the jackpot at a casino near her ski resort.*

Winter wedding

To do such an epic event, takes careful planning. Many high-end resorts supply a full-service planning menu, such as: Mammoth Mountain, Heavenly Mountain, Deer Valley, Squaw Valley, Beaver Creek, Whiteface Mountain, Vail Ski Resort, Copper Mountain, Steamboat Springs, Crested Butte, Arapahoe Basin, Winter Park Resort, Telluride Ski Resort, Keystone Ski Resort, Sugarbush Mountain, Breckenridge Ski Resort. The venue can be extensive or it can be tailored to your taste. They can plan a Bachelorette party, wedding, and post-wedding event (Honeymoon). The average number of guests attending the wedding is 250 people. The resorts have all kinds of packages besides room stay; they can accommodate ski rental, lift pass, private ski lesson, and other packages.

Photo 47. A Winter wedding and how lucky for all their guests who can stay over a few more days for skiing.

Keepsake for Memories

Many of the experiences that you will encounter will be once-in-a-lifetime event. You certainly want a professional photographer taking those memories for you and not just selfie photos. This is special, and if the event was special, you may want to obtain these special photographs.

Photo 48. With all the captured fun moments on and around the ski resorts do not miss any keepsake for a lifetime memories with a professional photographer.

Closure

As many have often said, "life's is short, I want to fill every second with adventure and fun." With that philosophy, don't just do a ski trip and return home empty handed without any photographs to share with friends and family. I have provided you with a robust list of fun and adventure activities that can amuse you and the family. Plan for it, research it, and book it! Fill your scrap book with fun- filled memories.

Photo 49. A Panoramic Scene.

THIS BOOK HAS ENOUGH IDEAS
TO MAXIMIZE YOUR VACATION
TRIP TO ADD INVALUABLE
MEMORIES AND VALUE THAT YOU
WON'T REGRET.

THE US Review of Books

5.0 ★★★★★

The Hidden Secrets and Treasures of Having Fun on and Around the Ski Resorts

by Dr. Herbert K. Naito

book review by Toby Berry

"Don't forget to rent a helmet to protect your noodle!"

Everyone knows that skiing can be fun. After all, it is a whole sports industry. But as the book illustrates, there is more for the asking at most ski areas. The theme here is to expand and explore adventure horizons. From activities as crazy and cold as ice yachting to more mellow and introspective alternatives like bird watching or yoga, Naito helps readers see the possibilities for a life well lived.

Naito is a medical professional, and all of his recreation books treat their subject matter holistically, making sure to include all the aspects a person should consider to make the activity most successful. His narrative makes it clear that a positive psyche is the first element of a good life. For example, it is great to go skiing, but the bigger picture involves broadening life's possibilities. One should be prepared and optimistic while embarking on some of the many adventures offered up at or around ski resorts.

Each suggested activity is described with a lively brief overview and a paragraph or two to set the scene. This may make readers want to do something that they never considered doing before, such as taking a hot air balloon ride on a crisp sunny day at sun rise. Naito notes that this is the safest form of aviation. Nike may say to just do it, but Naito helps readers figure out how, why, where, and when to go. Having fun is somewhat of a learned behavior. Thankfully, the author helps readers learn it.

9 798893 810851